T0355842

Praise for *Hurdle-isms*

"Any fragment of a sentence, any complete sentence, or any short paragraph that Coach says or writes, I want to learn. I anticipate that as you read this, you will feel the same."

—Buzz Williams
men's head basketball coach at Texas A&M

"Clint Hurdle is the embodiment of a true leader, someone who inspires and uplifts those around him. As a dear friend and mentor, Clint has always had the perfect words at the right time. I'm thrilled for anyone who picks up this book to experience the same wisdom and inspiration he's shared with me over the years."

—Sean Casey
former MLB player, coach, and analyst on MLB Network

"*Hurdle-isms* is an appropriate title for a man who had so many profound thoughts on baseball and life .... This highly entertaining and fun book provides a peek into the world of professional baseball at the highest level but with incredible life lessons that apply to your personal and professional life .... If you want life's lessons on CULTURE-LEADERSHIP-RELATIONS and what world class COMMUNICATION means and how it applies to everyday life, this book is a home run. Having known Clint for many years no one is more authentic and lives the life he talks about in the book than he does!! As you will read, like the game of baseball, there are two types of people: those who are humble and those who are about to be .... So do yourself a favor and find out why that is a good thing!! Enjoy learning from a transformational man who will make a transformational difference in your life!!!"

—Dan O'Dowd
former MLB general manager and analyst on MLB Network

"From his days as a rookie phenom on the cover of *Sports Illustrated* to his playing career, and years as coach, manager, and baseball adviser, Clint Hurdle has gathered and learned from experiences (including some highs and a few missteps) from which he has grown and used to guide others both on and off the field. His stories, wit, and wisdom make *Hurdle-isms* a must and enjoyable read for baseball fans and anyone looking to live a more effective and fulfilling life."

—Ron Shapiro
attorney, agent, *New York Times* best-selling author

"In *Hurdle-isms*, Clint artfully marries his endearing wit with his remarkable wisdom to bring the lessons that he has learned over his illustrious career to life. As a devout servant leader, Clint strives to enhance the lives of everyone he touches by magnanimously sharing his life's rich learnings from his successes and failures alike. Clint possesses the extraordinary ability to elevate the spirits of everyone in his orbit through his unflappable optimistic attitude and his authentic selflessness. As readers embrace Clint's *Hurdle-isms*, I am confident that he will prove to be a beacon of positivity as he has been for me throughout our 25-year friendship."

—Thad Levine
MLB executive

Clint Hurdle

Hurdle·isms

Wit and Wisdom
from a
Lifetime in Baseball

WILEY

Published by John Wiley & Sons, Inc., Hoboken, New Jersey.
Published simultaneously in Canada.

For general information on our other products and services or for technical support, please contact our Customer Care Department within the United States at (800) 762-2974, outside the United States at (317) 572-3993 or fax (317) 572-4002.

Wiley also publishes its books in a variety of electronic formats. Some content that appears in print may not be available in electronic formats. For more information about Wiley products, visit our web site at www.wiley.com.

Library of Congress Cataloging-in-Publication Data is Available:

ISBN 9781394292042 (Cloth)
ISBN 9781394292059 (ePub)
ISBN 9781394292066 (ePDF)

Cover Design: Paul McCarthy
Cover Art: © Shutterstock
Bat: Zhee-Graphic
Trim: 35Lab
SKY10097197_012725

There is one man who I want to dedicate this book to, and it's my dad: Big Clint. There are no Hurdle-isms without you.

Sixty-one years ago my dad asked me, "Do you want to go outside and play catch?"

I replied, "Catch what?"

Dad said, "A baseball."

My life hasn't been the same since because of my dad's love for the game. It was passed down to me, and I am still sharing my love for the game of baseball.

My dad has been a big part of my life through all the hard times. From birth until now! Ha-ha. We've done life together, and we have checked all the boxes for "what to do" and "what not to do."

He is my hero, and I've been his fan forever. He's been a good husband, a good dad, a good friend, and a huge resource for me and everyone he has met on his journey. Thank you is not close.

I love you, Dad.

Contents

Contents

Ready-Set-Go

Why would a 66-year-old guy think he could write a book? Let alone have life experiences that he could share that might make others laugh or learn from or lean into?

Well, why not?

Let me explain. Every year I pick a word and sell out to it. This is not like a bunch of New Year's resolutions that I kick to the curb by February. I pick a word that will help me be a better person wherever I go and whomever I'm with.

For 2023, my word was *grow*.

At the time, I didn't want to "settle" into my retirement years. I've been journaling for 36 years, and with daily emails, I've been helping others become the best version of themselves for 15 years.

So *Grow* it was. My first challenge? I decided it was time I joined Twitter/X and Instagram and committed myself to pushing out positive engagement and encouragement through media that were new to me. I've learned much from social media. "Hunt for good, and you'll find it. Hunt for bad, and you'll find it. Be light, bright, and polite" (my son Christian shared this with me and it originates with the author Josh Ochs and his book *Light, Bright and Polite*).

My next challenge to continue growing? To write a book. 😳

My goal was to provide readers with a book filled with "Hurdle-isms." These 25 Hurdle-isms are quotes, phrases, and one-liners that have been well received by my coworkers, peers, media, friends, and family over the years. This book is full of short chapters on hot topics, lessons learned, failures, and successes followed by the experience, strength, and hope gained. They might even make you laugh, and we all need laughter in our lives.

The Hurdle-isms

1. Don't keep score.
2. Shower well.
3. Get a good pitch to hit.

4. Multitasking makes me multi-mediocre.

5. You become great by being good for a long time.

6. Hard work doesn't guarantee success; however, not working hard will guarantee *not* having success.

7. Develop a white-belt mentality.

8. Let's drop this "old-school" versus "new-school" debate.

9. Not everything in life and sport needs to be leveraged.

10. Build your Mount Rushmore.

11. There are two kinds of people in this world: those who are humble and those who are about to be.

12. The smallest package in the world is a person wrapped up in themself.

13. Honored to serve. Humbled to help.

14. Build the house.

15. There's no guarantee you're going to get to sip lemonade by the pool.

16. I'm just trying to be a simple person in a complex world!

Ready-Set-Go

17. Lower the bar and you lose the winners; raise the bar and you lose the losers.

18. We don't have time to have "just another day."

19. Honor the exit.

20. Don't lose your stuff.

21. It's not about proving others wrong; it's about proving yourself right.

22. Model the behaviors you hope to instill in others.

23. Respect everyone, fear no one.

24. The tone and timing of what we say can be a deal-maker or a deal-breaker. Boom!

25. Celebrate others' success; when you celebrate others, you get to celebrate way more often.

When I read a book, I want to be told a story. I want the writer to paint me a picture. I tried to do that with each Hurdle-ism. I want you to say "I've done that, too!" or "I never thought of that!" or "Wow, I didn't see that coming!"

So let's open up this book and *grow* a little together!

During spring training, the team is getting to know each other as well as the staff. The coaching staff is assessing their organizational talent and depth. The games count, but they don't matter. It's time to have some fun and build momentum for the upcoming season. Let's play ball!

Chapter 1

Have Fun

You're going to succeed when you're having fun in life and when you take the time to focus on what you love doing. These Hurdle-isms are like when you create the roster in the spring to set you up for success in the season.

Hurdle-isms for Having Fun

- **Hurdle-ism 1:** Don't keep score.
- **Hurdle-ism 2:** Shower well.

Hurdle-ism 1: Don't Keep Score

I bet you're thinking: *What? For most of my life I've played sports, and the score definitely mattered! What do you mean, "Don't keep score"?*

My dad told me at a young age that all I needed to pay attention to so I could understand the game was to keep an eye on the scoreboard. The scoreboard would tell me everything important I needed to know about the game. I shared this with teammates all through Little League, Babe Ruth League, and American Legion baseball.

But as I got older and started playing at higher levels, I noticed the scoreboard started providing way more information than I thought necessary. Especially when it showed my batting average in big enough numbers for the entire stadium to see. If you're hitting well, it's no big deal. However, if you're not, it's an eyesore.

I started leaning into this idea of not keeping score later in my playing career as a way to simplify my approach to hitting. I would focus on the preparation, work hard in practice so I could "play" in the game, and control what I could control (which was effort and energy). And *not* focus on my batting average on the board.

We've all heard the catchphrases for peak performance, but it's hard to play baseball when your judge and jury is your batting average and when your self-esteem is tied directly to your level of performance.

As I became stubborn with this new approach and became steadfast with focusing on the quality of my preparation and reps, my game performance became better. My guts and heart were no longer tied to a base hit.

"Don't keep score" made perfect sense to me when I used it in this context, and I actually found more freedom to have fun in my baseball life.

Could this work in my personal life as well? Huh . . . you mean I should just do the right thing because it's the right thing to do? If someone asks me for a favor, I shouldn't document it and place it in a file to be brought up later when I would need a favor? You got to be kidding me; I was the king of keeping score!

You mean I need not judge others by their actions and stop judging myself by my intentions? I was also very good at that, too. Hey, you said you'd have that report to me by Friday and it's Friday! Meanwhile, I'm three days late on a project delivery; however, I've been busy because I'm a Big Deal.

5

Have Fun

Hey, I gave you a super cool and expensive Christmas present, and you gave me a book. Remember when we went to dinner and I picked up the bill and you gave me a dozen plain doughnuts as fair trade value? (Disclaimer: I do love plain doughnuts!)

Keeping score will wear you out, and you'll wear out everyone in your circle of friends.

There is only one person capable of keeping score of everybody's everythings, and He doesn't keep score.

Hurdle-ism 2: Shower Well

It was 2004, and our team in Colorado was not playing well at game time. We were streaking the wrong way, and losses were piling up.

Our pregame preparations were solid. Scout meetings, early work, and team and individual attention to detail all were all racing along. But during the games our tires were flat.

After one of the losses, our team president, Keli McGregor, strolled down to my office. I didn't know if he was there to provide support, vent disappointment, or just ask questions to get some answers.

There was no topic that was off-limits between me and Keli, so I was looking forward to getting his take on our slump. I tried to get him involved in baseball game strategy. Keli said he wasn't qualified. I looked him in the eye and said, "Neither am I, but I'm the manager." We laughed over that one quite frequently.

We challenged each other to be uncommon. Not common men, but uncommon. We wanted to truly make a difference. To create separation. To not be like everybody else. To not accept mediocrity. OK was not good enough.

Have Fun

So as we started to analyze what was happening and not happening on the field, Keli asked me to cut to the chase and give him one thought on what was next.

I looked him in the eye and said, "Shower well."

He asked me to explain. I shared that the game had done everything it could do to us today. We weren't able to meet its demands, and that was on me. Either we win or we learn. You only lose when you don't learn. So my advice to our organization was to "shower well."

In other words, wash the events of the day off. Watch them circle down the drain. Truly shampoo – rinse and repeat. Get the grime, dirt, disappointment, frustration, anxiety, and worry of today off of your body and mind and get them clean. Then go home and rest.

Keli nodded his head and said he liked that. He asked if he could use that metaphor with our employees. I said sure and then started thinking. . . .

"Shower well" works in life as well. Think about it. Bad day at work. Grumpy boss. Missed deadlines. No communication. They don't understand me. Bounced check. Lack of guidelines. Hard conversations. Traffic jams in rush hour. Flat tire. Need I go on? You get it.

So many real challenges happen every day to each one of us on our individual journeys. So much is out of our control. It can be overwhelming, like drinking from a firehose. I love that analogy because I've lived it. That is why my reset button has been and will continue to be "shower well." I get it all off me before I head home. I wash it all off me and get clean. I get ready for what's next.

Do you "shower well"? Give it a try. I think you'll be glad you did.

Have Fun

Chapter 2

Be Patient and Learn to Focus

I wasn't always a patient person. God kept giving me opportunities to develop my patience through trying times, but it takes a lot of courage to have patience. As I've gotten older, patience has become an acquired skill.

With patience comes a feeling of peace, which helps with focus. I finally got to a place where I could control my focus and eliminate all other distractions around me, taking one thing at a time.

Hurdle-isms for Being Patient and Learning to Focus

- **Hurdle-ism 3:** Get a good pitch to hit.
- **Hurdle-ism 4:** Multitasking makes me multi-mediocre.

Hurdle-ism 3: Get a Good Pitch to Hit

This gem took years to develop even though I probably heard it as a hitter a million times.

I've spent many years of my life trying to hit a baseball and trying to coach others who are trying to hit a baseball. After playing baseball, I became a manager in the New York Mets organization, and one of my responsibilities was to coach the hitters.

I later became a hitting coordinator for the Colorado Rockies organization for three years, and my job was to oversee six hitting coaches and close to 90 hitters.

I was a hitting coach in the Big Leagues for six years: five years in Colorado (1997–2002) and for one year in Texas (2010).

That's a lot of hitting and a lot of picking up baseballs. We were up early in the morning on the field and hitting in the cages.

If I were able to replay the video from all my base hits I had during my entire playing career, I suspect that more than 95% of them happened because I was able to "get a good pitch to hit."

I don't claim to be an expert on hitting; however, I've invested more time than most on helping hitters hit.

As a coach, I was constantly watching and reviewing swings. During the game (this was before in-game video analysis was available!), I was the voice of reason for hitters. Even after the emergence of video, one of my jobs was to earn the hitters' trust. I became "their eyes."

After each at bat most hitters will ask the hitting coach, "What did you see?"

As a coach, I needed to be concise and very clear with my communication and instruction if needed. There was a game going on. My response might not be what the hitter wanted to hear or the hitter might disagree with my assessment. In fact, it could get messy. This can get challenging when you are working with 8–12 hitters every game.

So many times as a hitter I found myself running down to first base after swinging at a pitch and not resonating what just happened, and I was hearing that from hitters as well. I was watching it on video during or after games, and I realized many outs are made because we don't "get a good pitch to hit."

13

Be Patient and Learn to Focus

After reviewing my process of in-game coaching, I came to the conclusion I needed to simplify the exchange of communication. So early in my hitting coach career, when a hitter came to me and asked, "What did you see?" my go-to question for him was "Did you get a good pitch to hit?" So many times that ended the conversation. If you don't "get a good pitch to hit," it's hard to get a hit. Getting a hit is a hard thing to do. I tried to keep it simple for them.

You can apply the question of "getting a good pitch to hit" to your life. Whatever task I take on, I ask myself if I am putting myself in a good position to succeed:

- Did I eliminate distractions?

- Did I prepare?

- Did I practice?

- Did I produce?

- Did I honestly self-evaluate my performance and see where there was room for improvement?

- Did I see the challenge correctly?

- Did I do my research before I shared my response?

- Did I reach out to others that might have gone through this situation to share their experiences?

I've swung at some bad pitches . . . so have you. That makes it hard to get a hit.

But one bad swing doesn't always end the at-bat. There is usually another opportunity to "get a good pitch" and deliver a hit.

Hitting is a lot like life. It can be simple but not easy.

Be Patient and Learn to Focus

Hurdle-ism 4: Multitasking Makes Me Multi-Mediocre

I can remember early in my managerial career reading an article on how multitasking was the newest superpower in leadership. I took notes on the article. I laid out a format to follow on the key points I pulled from the article. I reread the article. I tried to complete a couple of other tasks while reading the article again (which turned into a mess for me). I created an itinerary for my next day in which I would try to accomplish two tasks simultaneously filled by an afternoon exercise of attempting to complete three tasks simultaneously.

You can stop laughing now.

But I get it; the results of my multiple multitasking exercises were a joke.

Here's what I accomplished:

- Continual distractions mentally. I became a dog chasing a frisbee. I was chasing each thought without completing the original thought.

- I was forgetting where I was on one task when I attempted to return to it. I had no GPS system in place, and I became very good at getting lost. My recovery time was very slow. (Ask my wife, Karla, about my directional skills . . . she will laugh. I have none.)

- Every time I got lost mentally, I worked quicker, so I got lost faster. The same thing happens to me when I'm driving a car and make a wrong turn.

At the end of all of the multitasking, I was worn out and had actually accomplished zero. #fail

You might be a person who can multitask and do it well. God bless you! I do believe there are people who can. I am *not* one of them.

In hindsight, my weak attempt at multitasking turned into gold for me in my personal life and in my professional space. I was able to realize beyond a shadow of a doubt I was made to do one thing at a time. One.

I'm best served by putting my complete energy and focus into the task in front of me. No ifs, ands, or buts. One thing. One person. One conversation. One thought. One phone call.

This way I have the best chance of putting myself in the best position to make the best decision. To have the

Be Patient and Learn to Focus

best conversation. To have the best thought. To listen in the best manner.

Really, how annoying is it to be sitting across from someone and having a discussion when they are not 100% engaged? When they are distracted, are they listening to hear or are they listening to reply?

Eye contact is a game changer. Look into the eyes of the person you are speaking to. A faraway gaze usually means a faraway mind.

Do you have guts? Ask your wife, significant other, kids, and friends if they feel like the most important person in the room when you are with them.

I'm still working on one thing at a time/one day at a time (ODAAT). If you know where ODAAT originated, we have that in common. If you know, you know. I'm a work in progress who truly wants to be the best version of me to my family, my team, and all whom I connect with daily.

Part II
Summer

As a kid, summers were made for baseball. No school. Long days. We had the freedom to play all day long if we wanted to.

In pro ball, the summers are a big testing ground. The grind of daily heat or daily rain. Limited days off. You get into a routine that will test you physically, mentally, and emotionally. God, I love it!

Chapter 3

Put in the Hard Work

Showing up is half the battle. Doing the daily hard work is the other half. It all comes down to discipline. For me, self-discipline is a superpower. Once you're out on your own, every decision you make affects whether your next decision will be easier or harder. And without discipline, you will have regret.

Hurdle-isms for Putting in the Hard Work

- **Hurdle-ism 5:** You become great by being good for a long time.

- **Hurdle-ism 6:** Hard work doesn't guarantee success; however, not working hard will guarantee *not* having success.

Hurdle-ism 5: You Become Great by Being Good for a Long Time

Everyone wants to be great; however, most people don't have any idea how to make that happen.

Being great is hard, especially if greatness is your only end goal. I'm all in favor of having goals and striving for greatness. It's honorable, in fact. I'm a big fan of having people on my team who want to achieve greatness!

The challenge is in how you plan to arrive at greatness. In my life, I've encountered all shapes and sizes of people who are striving for greatness in many different walks of life. Obviously, I've seen this more in baseball than in any other industry.

We dream of it as kids. We play games in the backyard and on sandlots all across the nation. We re-create playoffs and World Series games as we put ourselves into the positions of Hall of Famers, most valuable players, and All-Stars. I believe it was Muhammad Ali who said, "If your dreams don't scare you, they're not big enough."

I thought I was great until I got into professional baseball. I was always the best player on my teams. I was a big fish in a small pond, and then in pro ball I became a small fish in a big pond.

I've seen so many players chase greatness, and rarely has the chase ended well when their focus has been on becoming great as soon as possible, mine included. I never became great. My journey became more of an obstacle course.

I was very successful early in my career. When I reached the Major Leagues, it was the first time that being great became the actual focus point. Earlier I just worked hard in practice so I could play in the game.

Now after a few good games, I would try to hit the "high-occupancy vehicle lane" and shoot into greatness. I'd try a little harder: I'd try to hit the ball a little farther, throw it a little farther, and so on. But by doing it that way, I soon lost the traction I had when I was "just" being good. I was too focused on trying to be great and not on being consistently good, day after day.

I didn't realize the error of my ways until my playing time was reduced greatly and I was playing off the bench more than starting. Shoot, being good for one day in the big leagues is hard. Being good for a week is harder.

Put in the Hard Work

Being good for a month is really good, and being good for a year is a tremendous accomplishment.

So, I started to focus on being good just for today. If I was, check. Enjoy the day. When tomorrow arrives, be good again . . . for that day. Stack the good days. Good days can turn into good weeks, which can turn into good months, which can turn into good years!

My good friend Todd Helton, who is in the Major League Baseball Hall of Fame, would be the first to tell you his goal was to be good today and let the rest of it take care of itself.

You become great by being good for a long time.

This belief is true in everyday life as well. You don't become a great parent, a great mom, a great dad, a great brother, a great sister, or a great friend overnight. You won't be a great employee or a great boss in a week. It will take you longer than a month to become a great mentor, leader, coach, or teacher. A good consistent year of day-to-day solid, consistent performance will put you in a position to be trusted, to be listened to, and to make a difference and impact others on the journey.

Be "good" today so you can become great tomorrow.

Hurdle-ism 6: Hard Work Doesn't Guarantee Success; However, Not Working Hard Will Guarantee *Not* Having Success

My first manager in pro ball was Gary Blaylock. A few years down the road I came to the conclusion he was the perfect first manager for me. Gary was all about hard work, and his thinking was that anyone can work hard when they felt like it or when things were going well, but the truly elite worked hard just because it was what was necessary every day.

He shared with me that hard work separated players at every level. If you were a ball player, you were expected to work hard just like you got grits with breakfast in the South – you got grits just because, and you worked hard just because.

Gary also shared the fact that working hard could become contagious. It starts with one player, and then a couple more players want to work hard. And then a few more will get on board. Then working hard becomes your team's mentality. You all roll up your sleeves and go to work.

Put in the Hard Work

Hard work doesn't guarantee success; however, not working hard will guarantee *not* having success. So work hard and you've got a chance. Don't work hard, and you'll be home soon.

We know that hard work alone doesn't guarantee success. However, if you know you put in the work, then it's one thing you don't have to wonder about when you don't perform well. There are other parts of the game that need to be done well for a team, let alone a player, to have success.

I've always believed that my confidence going into a game was best served by having done the hard work. Fear can creep into anyone's mindset when we know we haven't done all the work and we haven't prepared. We can fool other people about what we've done to prepare, but the guy in the mirror knows. And when you're in the clubhouse with your teammates, some of them will know as well.

Many players also do their work when others aren't watching. They don't need to be seen nor do they care what others think. Their self-esteem and self-confidence are not swayed by the thoughts or observations of others outside their sphere of influence.

Hurdle-isms

The other team has a say in what happens during the game and in regard to the final outcome. We all want to win. We all know it takes a personal commitment from every player on the team, and if you have a team of players committed to one another and are committed to working hard, you and your team are in the best position to have success.

Again, hard work doesn't guarantee success, but not working hard will guarantee *not* having success. You think this Hurdle-ism is true in your personal life?

Try not working hard in these areas:

- Any relationship
- Your marriage
- Your family time
- Your calendar management
- Returning calls, texts, or emails
- Your finances

Not working hard at any of those is a recipe for failure.

Work hard. You'll be glad you did and so will everyone you love.

Chapter 4

Be a Lifelong Learner

I once heard a saying that "youth is wasted on the young." I think I pretty much epitomized that quote in my younger years; however, once I realized that my learning should never stop, I developed a thirst for knowledge and learning new things.

As Toby Keith would sing, "Don't let the Old Man in." No one likes a "know it all" that doesn't really know anything at all.

Hurdle-isms for Being a Lifelong Learner

- **Hurdle-ism 7:** Develop a white-belt mentality.
- **Hurdle-ism 8:** Let's drop this "old-school" versus "new-school" debate.

- **Hurdle-ism 9:** Not everything in life and sport needs to be leveraged.

- **Hurdle-ism 10:** Build your Mount Rushmore.

Hurdle-ism 7: Develop a White-Belt Mentality

I first heard this phrase during my time with two very good friends of mine in the Pittsburgh Pirates organization, our Director of Mental Skills, Bernie Holliday, and our Assistant General Manager and Director of Player Development, Kyle Stark.

These were big titles for guys much younger than me and smarter than me. There was no doubt in my mind I was going to be able to lean into these men and learn about much more than baseball.

One day Bernie told the story of a great judo teacher and champion who was in his last days of life and who shared with those he was mentoring that he wanted to be buried in his white belt. His younger disciples were appalled. The most accomplished judo master of all time most certainly should be buried in his black belt, they all agreed. He shook his head. "No, I entered this world a 'white belt,' and I want to enter my next world as a 'white belt.' I will always strive to be a lifelong learner."

Be a Lifelong Learner

That man was authentic and knowledgeable and was teaching his disciples until the end. How about if we could all get dipped in that kind of understanding of life?

My son, Christian, reinforced this lesson during his time in karate class. He was embarking on a new sport, after having retired from baseball at the age of four (isn't that ironic?) and spending some time dabbling in tennis. Christian is creative and sees life through a unique lens. He shared with me he would be getting his uniform (obi) soon and was excited to show me and Karla.

Sure enough, he arrived from practice with his arms full. He put on his robe and started showing me some moves he had learned. He was throwing hands and delivering kicks to an imaginary object all with his robe open. I asked him if that was hard to do without a belt. He then remembered he had forgotten to tighten his obi with the belt and went to retrieve it.

Once he had his belt in place and secured, Christian asked me if I knew what the white belt stood for. As a father, you sometimes play along and let your children teach you something they have learned, right? Of course, I knew what a white belt stood for, I said to myself. It means you know nothing and are starting from the bottom to work your way up. Duh!

Now – wait for it – Christian told me the white belt was the best belt because you had a chance to learn everything!

Mic drop!

Or was that my jaw hitting the ground? Christian just spoke his wisdom into me, and that moment still sticks to me like glue today. Oh, to see life through the eyes of a child.

From that day on, I've shared the white-belt mentality in clubhouses, board rooms, and C-suites.

How many people in your sphere of influence have a white-belt mentality?

I've been sharing positivity and encouragement through texts and emails since 2009, and Christian (now 19) and our family's best friend Alex Hritz encouraged me to get my messaging out on a larger platform. As I mentioned in the Ready-Set-Go section, I sauntered into the Wild Wild West of social media in 2023: Instagram, Facebook, LinkedIn, and X.

Christian gave me three rules of engagement: be light, be bright, and be polite. If someone hates on you, just go

Be a Lifelong Learner

away. Don't engage or try to win an imaginary argument. (It doesn't seem like everyone else got that memo on X!)

I've also taken on this challenge and journey of writing a book. I've had many people reach out over the last 20 years and ask if I'd come alongside them and share my story. It never seemed like a good idea to me while I was managing a baseball team. It required too much time, energy, and effort from my perspective.

Now that I'm semiretired, I decided that it's time. So here I am still learning.

Our friend Alex has a saying for our dogs when their behavior is less than human. "They're still learning" has become a common theme in our home for our dogs as well as for myself. I still have a chance to learn so much more in this life, and I'm thankful and grateful for those who are guiding me. I need to use my ears and eyes to learn . . . not my mouth.

Hurdle-ism 8: Let's Drop This "Old-School" Versus "New-School" Debate

This Hurdle-ism started unfolding for me back when I was the manager of the Pittsburgh Pirates. Our general manager (GM) was Neal Huntington, who had graduated from Amherst and had developed his baseball IQ in Montreal and Cleveland. Neal had some good mentors along the way; he also was a tireless worker with a brilliant mind and had a deep passion for baseball and those who played it.

His baseball IQ is high, and he was one of the forerunners of the analytical approach to the game. He had also brought in two super-sharp guys to help install and develop our Department of Analytics and Research: Dan Fox and Mike Fitzgerald. To say they got my attention with the analytics that could be used in the game would be an understatement.

When the four of us would sit down, my mere high school education came up a little short. But what I could bring to the table was experience. I had experience with people within the game and a perspective from the

Be a Lifelong Learner

playing field, dugout, and clubhouse consisting of more than 35 years at the time.

To say I bought in right away would be a flat-out lie. Actually, it took me two years in Pittsburgh to actually understand all the different metrics and what they meant and which ones to value most.

After the 2012 season, Neal and I scheduled a meeting at my home in Pittsburgh. We had two seasons when there were signs of improvement that had ended harshly. In both seasons we had solid first halves just to fall way short in the second halves. We needed to recalibrate our model for success.

So that day at my house Neal and I spent at least six hours reviewing all the aspects of our development program for our Major League team. We discussed, argued, collaborated, and shared our thoughts and what we each felt were the proper next steps. We truly became a partnership that day.

I got on board with becoming analytically driven, and we agreed we would honor the human analytics of the game as well. Neal showed me that learning and implementing new strategies can be exciting and rewarding. I'm forever thankful and grateful for that day.

We need to drop this "old-school" versus "new-school" conflict that often occurs – whether it's in sports, politics, or religion. It seems like everyone has to take a side. You're right, and they're wrong. Stop it! Let's all just be "in school" together. Let's ask, what can we learn from each other? What can we teach each other?

Two men with the same goal and different ways to accomplish the goal threw their egos out the door and decided to do what we believed would build a winning ball team in Pittsburgh – this on the heels of our 20th consecutive losing season. A "new-school" GM and an "old-school" manager decided to be in school with each other and lock arms and commit to our organization and to each other.

Did it work?

We made the playoffs the next three seasons and snapped the 20-year losing streak as well as the 21 years without a playoff game. We were able to reunite a city's bond with its baseball team – a goal I shared publicly years before when named manager in November 2010.

And since then, this Hurdle-ism has become a rallying cry of mine, especially since 2019. When I was fired by Pittsburgh on November 13, 2019, I said I was putting the

Be a Lifelong Learner

uniform in the closet and signing with the home team: my family. I took two years off and then was given the opportunity to rejoin the Rockies organization in 2021.

When I returned to Colorado, the game of baseball had a facelift. It seemed that human analytics had lost value and were being replaced by more statistical analytics than the game had ever seen.

"Old-school" versus "new-school" was becoming a fistfight on paper and with personnel. It was going on at all levels as well. I've come to realize that when I fail at something, if given a second chance, I overcorrect. Our game was going through this phase in my eyes because our game had gotten boring. The three absolutes – home run, strikeout, and walk – were all that was going on. I agreed we needed to do something. The analytics became staples, and the touch and feel for the game dissipated.

More recently, though, we've seen a recalibration. We are not as much "new school," and we are revisiting "old school" techniques. And I see many organizations becoming "in school." I truly believe the best organizations in sport and business are a hybrid model and incorporate analytical evaluations with human evaluations.

Hurdle-isms

We need the reminder that humans play the game, and humans have a heartbeat. So does the game. You eliminate the heart, you lose the human. You eliminate the heart from the game, and you get a stale game played in a vacuum. I'm going to stay "in school." How about you?

Hurdle-ism 9: Not Everything in Life and Sport Needs to Be Leveraged

The word *leverage* has become a buzzword in sports since the early 2010s. I don't think it was even a part of my vocabulary until the beginning of my tenure in Pittsburgh. According to Wikipedia, *leverage* is defined as "to use something that you already have in order to achieve something new or better."

In baseball terms, it means to have the upper hand of a situation, or the percentages of success are in your favor.

The game of baseball now has leverage opportunities from beginning to end. You have the option of using an "opener" to start the game followed by a "bulk reliever" to get you (if you have the lead) to your "bridge" relievers to get to the "closer." It's a lot to consider.

You can leverage your lineup throughout the game by using multiple pinch hitters in different situations to capitalize on a leverage opportunity. What we've done is create a game in which we try to leverage (or win) every single confrontation between pitcher and hitter.

Instead, players should have the opportunity to fail and learn from adversity. We can't follow our kids around all day and catch them before they fall, nor should we. Falling and failing are a part of life. You really haven't failed unless you stop trying.

Most of the players in professional sports have trained for the "big moments" throughout their careers. Most pros want to have the opportunity to get the job done at crunch time. As a coach and manager, I had the extreme pleasure of watching Larry Walker, Todd Helton, and Vladimir Guerrero (all Hall of Famers) as they embraced the situation and the challenge and were looking to come through for their teammates to help win the game. There were other players I coached or managed who were a joy to watch in extreme competition as well. Michael Young, Josh Hamilton, Nelson Cruz, and Ian Kinsler in Texas as well as Andrew McCutchen, Russell Martin, and A. J. Burnett in Pittsburgh were all fierce competitors.

There will always be lessons learned in those moments. Did I try too hard? Did I breathe and relax? Did I embrace the feelings and the noise of the crowd? Was I overwhelmed by all of it?

Then when the opportunity is over and you've done the job, the confidence that can come from the experience

Be a Lifelong Learner

is huge. It can help you when moving forward. You've been there and done that.

If you come up short, there can be experience gained as well and being able to lean into the disappointment and be grateful for the belief your boss or manager showed in you by giving you the chance. You can also share the experience with your coaches and teammates about what you took away from it. Was I prepared for the moment? Did I train well for the moment? Once I was in the moment, did I rely on my training and just play and love every second of the confrontation?

What lessons can be learned from not trying to leverage every situation in life?

I won't speak for you; however, I will share that most times I've intentionally tried to leverage a situation in life, the end result has been less than favorable. You don't need to leverage a date. You don't need to leverage school or sporting opportunities for your kids. I don't believe you need to leverage an interview for a job.

From my experience, things happen best when they unfold organically. I really do believe we are prepared for our future if we've paid attention to our past.

Adversity can be a wonderful teacher.

Those who become elite in their given profession continually speak of defining moments of challenge and failure. I'm still amazed by having had a front-row seat watching the performances under pressure by George Brett, Hal McRae, Johnny Bench, Tom Seaver, Ozzie Smith, Gary Carter, and Keith Hernandez as teammates. We should also continue to push ourselves outside our comfort zones and embrace new technologies and techniques.

43

Be a Lifelong Learner

Hurdle-ism 10: Build Your Mount Rushmore

In 2011, when I was the manager of the Pittsburgh Pirates, we started the season strong but ended poorly, the team's 19th consecutive losing season. And the next year? We had the longest seasonal losing streak in North American sports history . . . ouch.

With such a tough position to be in, I needed to have a system of checks and balances in place for my focus and vision to be undistracted and maintain a healthy rhythm. As a lifelong learner, I would need help.

My wife, Karla, is my first sounding board, and I also have a posse of people in my life whom I lean into when I'm stuck or looking for answers. I've learned the hard way that asking for help is a superpower and that I'll never have all the right answers. I need to surround myself at home and at the ballpark with people I trust, and I know they will speak truth to me.

I don't need bobbleheads to ask for advice or to ask what I'm missing.

It was my friend Rod Olson who encouraged me to come up with a Mount Rushmore group of people to connect with – a group I knew I could trust. I knew they cared about me, and I knew they could make me better. We also knew we could call on each other at any time with no judgment and share what was on our mind or what challenges we were walking through.

My friend Mike Matheny, former Major League manager of the Kansas City Royals and St. Louis Cardinals, also spoke wisdom to me along the same lines. Mike called it having a board of directors for your life.

Both men stated the importance of having people who weren't like me as part of my team – people who are in different lines of work but with similar responsibilities and roles so there was an understanding of the chain of command. One of me is more than enough, and I learn more from people with different back stories than mine.

Be a Lifelong Learner

Part III

All-Star Break

The All-Star Break is like a cold glass of water on a really hot day. It's a time to pause, rest, reflect, and plan. I would always use a "traffic light" exercise at the break for my team and for myself. It goes like this: a traffic light has three lights:

- **Red:** Stop.
- **Yellow:** Proceed with caution.
- **Green:** Go.

I assigned these traffic lights to questions that I asked myself and that the players could ask themselves to improve during the break:

- **Red:** What do I/we need to stop doing?

- **Yellow:** What do I/we need to reevaluate with clarity?

- **Green:** What do I/we need to continue to do?

Then, for the most part, it was time to turn off the noise of the season.

Chapter 5

Be Humble

$\mathbf{M}$y mind has always battled a tug of war between "It's not about me" versus "It's all about me." For example, when I returned home from a road trip, sometimes I would be waiting for the welcoming parade to acknowledge my return when I should have just returned quietly and fell back into the family routine happy to be back into the flow.

I've come to the realization that humility is one of the best traits a successful person can have. As you might have heard, humility does not mean thinking less of yourself. It means thinking of yourself less.

In fact, people who are really good at something usually will never tell you how good they are at that something. For example, George Brett, Larry Walker, and Todd Helton – all with 300+ home runs and career batting averages over 0.300 – never told me how good they were at playing baseball. Yet all three of them are in Cooperstown in the Baseball Hall of Fame.

Hurdle-isms for Being Humble

- **Hurdle-ism 11:** There are two kinds of people in this world: those who are humble and those who are about to be.

- **Hurdle-ism 12:** The smallest package in the world is a person wrapped up in themself.

- **Hurdle-ism 13:** Honored to serve. Humbled to help.

Hurdle-ism 11: There Are Two Kinds of People in This World: Those Who Are Humble and Those Who Are About to Be

In 1978 during my rookie year in Kansas City, I spent many hours under the tutelage of our hitting coach Charley Lau. By then Charley had established himself as one of the premier hitting coaches in the history of baseball. Many players found their best swings with Charley, and the fact that Kansas City Royals stars George Brett and Hal McRae were disciples of Charley added to his street cred. George went on to become one of the best players and hitters in Major League Baseball history and was inducted in the Hall of Fame in 1999, and Hal was one of the best hitters in the American League for many years. They were two tremendous teammates and friends as well.

I spent many hours working with Charley that season. His eye for the swing and his professorial demeanor added to his quiet but confident personality. I don't remember any time that he raised his voice when teaching or coaching unless it was in an uproar of approval.

Be Humble

During that first year, I was having an incredibly challenging time with my consistency in the batter's box. Some weeks I was hitting like I invented the game, and other weeks I couldn't hit water if I fell out of a boat. It was truly a roller coaster ride for myself and my emotions.

After one of my best offensive weeks of the season, I was awarded the American League Player of the Week Award, which came with a Bulova watch. It had the American League insignia on the dial and an inscription on the back with my name, team, and the week of the season.

At the ceremony to receive the watch at a homestand about a month later, I was just about to walk on the field in front of the fans to accept the award when Charley put his arm around me and said, "I'm proud of you, Clint. Always remember, there are two types of people in this world: those who are humble, and those who are about to be. You've been both. Remain the first one."

I wish I could say I learned that lesson my rookie year and never looked back; however, that would be very far from the truth.

I've heard the beauty of life is that you get lessons one at a time. When you learn the lesson that life presents you, you become a wiser person. If you don't learn the particular lesson the first time, you get that lesson again, presented differently, until you do learn it. And once you learn that lesson, then you receive the reward of getting another lesson. I've learned a lot of lessons and been humbled each time I do. So I'm here to tell you that I don't want to be the person who "is about to be" anymore.

I've pretty much had the ego kicked out of me, and it's been replaced with humility.

Be Humble

Hurdle-ism 12: The Smallest Package in the World Is a Person Wrapped Up in Themself

Geeesh. This chapter on humility is making me revisit some challenging times. There are variations of the quote "The smallest package in the world is a person wrapped up in themself," with some versions attributed to Benjamin Franklin, but I first heard it in a Prader-Willi Syndrome (PWS) dad's group as we were discussing some hard feelings, and I knew I had to adopt it as a Hurdle-ism.

PWS is the birth defect my daughter Maddie was born with. It's a deletion of the 15th chromosome, which affects a person's satiation. For example, most people go through stages of being hungry to becoming full, but Maddie is hungry from the time she wakes up until the time she goes to sleep. The syndrome also affects her gross motor skills and her fine motor skills, and the IQ of a person with PWS most often plateaus in the 70–80 range. She is now 22 years old; however, in many areas Maddie functions as a 12-year-old.

The other fathers and I were sharing the ups and downs of our home lives. Everything changes when you have a special needs child. You need to find time for your wife and help her as much and as often as you can. You also need to find time for your other children because you don't want the entire family dynamic to revolve around doctor appointments and therapies.

One of the presentations at group was based on the lesson that this disability "isn't about you" and it "didn't happen to you." The point was we needed to eliminate thinking of ourselves only. I realized then that my family needed me to be a servant and to truly become selfless. It was the only way for my marriage to have meaning and for my children to thrive, each in their own ways.

Directly after the session was when I first heard "The smallest package in the world is a person wrapped up in themselves," and it has become my fight song from that point on. I've shared it with other fathers whom I have relationships with. I've shared it with other coaches I've met. I've shared it with players I work with.

I live my best life when I share from the inside out and give my time, talent, or attention freely.

55

Be Humble

Karla needs a husband. Our children need a father. My friends need a friend. When I'm wrapped up in myself, my job, or my hobbies, I'm a very selfish person. I'm really of no service to anybody, and that makes me cringe. I've been that person, and it's a very lonely place to be.

Hurdle-ism 13: Honored to Serve. Humbled to Help

I was surprised the first time I wrote "Honored to served. Humbled to help." because I actually meant every word. But when they're true, it's the best way to be a part of something.

It was after the National League playoffs in 2007. I was manager of the Colorado Rockies, and we had won the play-in game versus the San Diego Padres in dramatic fashion. We had finished the season with identical records and were forced into a one-game "win-or-go-home" scenario. An epic slide by outfielder Matt Holliday into home plate and a safe call by the home plate umpire Tim McClelland turned Coors Field and the downtown area known as "LoDo" into an absolute frenzy.

The team then went on to win seven straight play-off games. We marched through the National League Division Series versus the Philadelphia Phillies and the Arizona Diamondbacks. We were headed toward the World Series as National League Champions!

There was only one problem . . . there was no one to play.

The Cleveland Indians and the Boston Red Sox went through a seven-game gauntlet in which the Red Sox battled back from a 3–1 deficit to become the American League champions.

We had to wait eight days to start the World Series.

Our team had just put on one of the best September finishes of all time. We had won 20 out of 21 games and had more than adrenaline on our side . . . until we had to wait and watch . . . and wait and watch.

We ended up losing the 2007 World Series to the Red Sox. They were hot and talented, and the wait didn't do us any favors.

As I was writing an end-of-season letter to our team president, Keli McGregor, I closed with these words: "Honored to serve. Humbled to help."

It was true. I had never been part of such an incredible organizational success before. I had never been part of such a huge team accomplishment: it took us 163 games, but our entire organization celebrated it together. It took the effort of every coach and player as well as every employee for us to push our way through five hard seasons together. I was the manager, but I was only one small part of a priceless memory for everyone in the Rockies

Major League Organization and player development system and for all of our professional and amateur scouts.

"Honored to serve. Humbled to help." There's that word *humble* again. It's a wonderful feeling when you can be a small part of something that brings so much joy to so many people on so many different levels.

If you approach your job as a way to provide service to others and not to be the most important person in the chain of command, you will be fulfilled.

Chapter 6

Navigate the Ups and Downs in Life Like a Champ

L ife does not happen in a linear fashion. I don't think anything in my life has happened in a straight line – outside of me getting older, that is. The warranty on some of my parts is starting to expire!

All of these zigs-and-zags have come with a fair share of up and downs, with many of the downs self-inflicted. Just to name a few:

- I was a can't-miss prospect who missed.
- Was traded, released, and fired (three times each!).
- Unfortunately earned two driving under the influences.
- I am twice divorced.

Have I captured your attention? I'm not proud of any of these low moments in my life; however, they're all part of my story.

Still, I have also been blessed beyond measure in many ways. Let me share a few:

- I've been happily married since 1999.

- I've been sober since 1998 (no coincidence in those dates!).

- I'm the father to three children.

- I've spent almost 50 years in professional baseball.

- I've been a Major League Baseball player, coach, or manager for more than 30 years.

- I've made three trips to the World Series.

I've also recommitted my life to Christ, and believe I've become the man God wants me to be: a good son, a good husband, a good father, a good friend, and a good teammate.

I believe honest self-evaluation is a superpower.

I can truly appreciate all of these highs because I've had all of the lows. I appreciate happy because I've been sad.

I appreciate friendship because I've been lonely. I appreciate having because I've not had. I appreciate bounce backs because I've had setbacks.

Life can be like a roller coaster. That's why you're advised to wear a seatbelt. You might need a helmet at times, too!

Hurdle-isms for Navigating Ups and Downs in Life Like a Champ

- **Hurdle-ism 14:** Build the house.
- **Hurdle-ism 15:** There's no guarantee you're going to get to sip lemonade by the pool.
- **Hurdle-ism 16:** I'm just trying to be a simple person in a complex world!

Hurdle-ism 14: Build the House

During my managerial time with the Colorado Rockies, we were forced to make some tough financial decisions with our roster. Our strategy was to move out higher paid players, try to acquire younger players, and bring up some of our drafted players and develop them at the Major League level. In any industry, going through a rebuilding period can be hard. It's hard on players, coaches, employees, sponsors, and fans.

The task can be overwhelming . . . and truthfully sometimes a little demoralizing.

The manager needs to find something the staff can rally around. With that in mind, I came up with the idea to share that we were going to "build the house." I was hoping to create a mindset where we didn't focus on what we didn't have and instead focused on what we *did* have.

We needed to be part of the group who laid a solid foundation that could withstand challenges. We were going to also encourage our team to play for the name on the front of the jersey – the team name – as well as the name on the back. We would teach solid fundamentals and remind everyone that we wanted to be extraordinary at the ordinary.

In these tough times, we would "build the house" and focus on each task at hand, not be consumed with the past. Our job as coaches was to work our players hard at practice so they could play during the game.

We focused on one day at a time. Then good days turned into good weeks, and good weeks turned into good months. Our steady approach to the daily tasks kept us from looking for distractions on the time line or comparing ourselves with other teams. We didn't need to look at other houses and wonder what types of materials were being used or how much money was being spent over there.

We just focused on the day-to-day job of building the house. We did look forward to the day the house would be built, but that doesn't mean we were guaranteed to be sipping lemonade by the pool once it was built. And that takes me to the next Hurdle-ism.

Navigate the Ups and Downs in Life Like a Champ

Hurdle-ism 15: There's No Guarantee You're Going to Get to Sip Lemonade by the Pool

During the most trying days of our building phase in Colorado (see Hurdle-ism 14), I would periodically get asked about my thoughts on my job security. One day I shared with our staff – and possibly the media – that I had signed up to build the house and wasn't really thinking about anything past that.

I said something like "There's no guarantee that I'm going to get to sip lemonade by the pool in the backyard."

What I meant was, I was going to stay focused on doing my job every day and not worry about whether I was here to reap any future rewards . . . like the builder who finally finishes the structural elements of their house but isn't necessarily the one living in the house, relaxing by the pool, barbequing hamburgers, and sipping lemonade.

In the sports world, I've always believed those who spend time worrying about money and their contracts should be worried, because these distractions keep them from doing their job to the best of their abilities.

This strategy of daily focus would give us a chance to achieve our vision of championship baseball. We ended up blazing a trail that others could follow in any organization. At the time, I didn't know that part of the endgame for us was going to be an incredible finish to a National League Championship and a trip to the 2007 World Series.

I applied this "lemonade by the pool" mentality in Pittsburgh, and it helped lead us to consecutive playoff appearances from 2013 to 2015 after having 20 consecutive losing seasons and 21 years without a playoff game.

These are just some examples of how I would much rather put my energy into building a solid house with a strong foundation than be doing backflips off the pool deck and have it all come crumbling down.

Navigate the Ups and Downs in Life Like a Champ

Hurdle-ism 16: I'm Just Trying to Be a Simple Person in a Complex World!

Have you ever listened to the song "Simple Man" by Lynyrd Skynyrd? It tells a powerful story through the lyrics of a mother's proclamation to her son to keep the main thing the main thing in life. It means put your focus on real things in life and be a person of truth, integrity, and courage.

Toward the end of the 2002 Major League Baseball season, I was worn out. I was finishing up my first year as a Major League manager, and it was taking its toll on me. I had managed six seasons in the New York Mets organization as a Minor League manager, and I felt I had learned many of the lessons I would need to become a Major League manager.

Boy . . . I had gotten a surprise that first season.

Don't get me wrong, I needed every one of those seasons and every lesson and lineup that came with it. However, there is no simulation for Major League Baseball and the daily grind you have with a new family and a daughter living away from you.

Maddie arrived in August 2002. As I mentioned, my little girl was born with a birth defect called Prader-Willi Syndrome, and the doctor and therapy appointments were filling our days, while baseball games were filling our nights. Ashley, my oldest daughter, was in her senior year of high school in California, and there were challenges with us being apart. I was tired.

I reached out to a friend, and after a long conversation, I decided to simplify my goals for the day: I consolidated my long to-do list into one item.

When I woke up in the morning, I said a prayer: "Lord. Help me become a simple person in a complex world." That's it. I was going to stop focusing on the 34 things on my to-do list and was just going to take care of the tasks in front of me one by one. By taking each day and each to-do item as it came, I was less mentally stressed when the schedules of doctor appointments, family obligations, and baseball games all collided.

This might not sound like a big change, but by seeing less in front of me, I was better served dealing with the task at hand. At first it was challenging to slow down and just focus on the task in front of me. Then it became more of a rhythm, and eventually it became a habit.

Navigate the Ups and Downs in Life Like a Champ

When everything is going great, it can be exciting to be so busy. But when you have a difficult task ahead of you, sometimes the only way to achieve it is to simplify it. I can remember when I arrived in Pittsburgh to manage the Pirates in 2011, and I was tasked with the enormous challenge of helping to turn around an organization that had 18 consecutive losing seasons. I was often asked how we were going to do it.

I replied with my own question (I can hear my sixth-grade English teacher Dorothy Duncan reminding me how unacceptable that was). I would ask back then, "How do you eat an elephant?" I would get mostly stares back, and then I would answer, "One bite at a time."

My "trying to be a simple person in a complex world" made sense to me, and by eliminating distractions and by keeping things simple, I developed a rhythm for the ups and downs in life that I've continued to this day.

Hurdle-isms

Part IV
Fall

I love fall baseball! The months of September and October are the best months to finish strong. The weather turns from hot to not. The colors on the trees and the trips to the ballpark are radiant.

Your finish can have a substantial impact on your overall season. We've all heard the phrase "It's not how you start; it's how you finish," and there is truth in that in baseball. However, if you start extremely well, you might not have to finish with a flurry.

No matter how your season has gone, finishing strong has so much upside. If your season has gone well to this point, it's a chance to create separation from the other teams and to ignite your fan base. It's also a chance to prepare for the playoffs.

If your season has been average, it's a chance to finish strong and catapult into playoff contention and end with fireworks.

If your season has been a hard one, it's a chance to evaluate overall talent and assess younger players by giving them more opportunities and reps. It's also a chance to create some positive energy and traction going into the offseason and to honestly self-evaluate staff and your player pool.

Chapter 7

Have a High Standard

This chapter is called "Have a High Standard." Read that again. It does not say have a standard that is unrealistic or have a standard that will drive you crazy to attain it.

My belief is that we should maintain standards in all things that we would need accountability, dependability, and responsibility to attain. They should be standards that we would also need to lean into others for support, feedback, and help to achieve. That is the high standard that I am talking about – high but attainable.

My desire is to set a standard that I can live up to and that others can depend on me to attain.

Mike Tomlin, the head coach of the Pittsburgh Steelers, has a mantra that he preaches at all times: "The standard is the standard."

I asked my good friend, Kevin Colbert, former Pittsburgh Steelers general manager, what this meant, and he replied, "Clint, when Mike references 'The Standard,' he is talking about the past and the present. He always talks about being appreciative of those who set the 'Steeler Standard' in the '70s while recognizing [the original owners] the Rooney family for their consistent platform back then and now. He challenges the current team to live up to it no matter the circumstance."

Kevin continued, "It was there before we got here, we might have added to it, and now we've got to match and exceed what we are all a part of. Shortened version: don't hide from The Standard you helped to create." That sums it up for me.

Hurdle-isms for Having a High Standard

- **Hurdle-ism 17:** Lower the bar and you lose the winners; raise the bar and you lose the losers.

- **Hurdle-ism 18:** We don't have time to have "just another day."

Hurdle-ism 17: Lower the Bar and You Lose the Winners; Raise the Bar and You Lose the Losers

In 2018, I was the manager of the Pittsburgh Pirates, and the new strength and conditioning coach, Jim Malone, had a whiteboard in the weight room that said, "Lower the bar and you lose the winners; raise the bar and you lose the losers." I immediately let Jim know I was borrowing this quote for the rest of my life. I've used it more times than I can count in more ways than I can count since then.

Jim and I had known each other for more than 10 years prior to him becoming a Pirate. He had worked for the San Diego Padres for many years, and we would frequent the same breakfast spot in the Gaslamp District. Cafe 222 was the place I went for food and focus. Jim seemed to be looking for the same. (Or we were both just hungry and had similar tastes!) When we were interviewing for a new strength and conditioning coach in Pittsburgh, Jim's name was on my list, and after interviewing all the candidates he was our choice.

Have a High Standard

It's been my experience, personally and professionally, that winners don't want to settle for less. They are consistently looking for ways to improve and get better physically and mentally. They don't want to be graded on a curve or work hard to become average or to be just OK.

A slogan that's not posted in a clubhouse or on a whiteboard: "Let's be OK." I understand there are days that OK is the best you've got. However, when you can look around the room into each other's eyes and see your teammate coming up short, you can raise him up. That's what good teams do. That's what good teammates do. There are no weak links.

By raising the bar, you continue to keep everyone's attention. By lowering the bar, you lose the attention and commitment level of the winners. They know you are lowering the bar and settling for less. As the leader, you also are the first one to know when you are lowering expectations and pivoting away from giving your best when your best is needed.

On that third Tuesday in July, when you've played close to 100 games, are you still raising the bar or lowering the bar? Your team will know. If you're lowering the bar, you might as well start waving a white flag, too.

Hurdle-ism 18: We Don't Have Time to Have "Just Another Day"

I believe it was spring training 2012 when I coined this Hurdle-ism. For whatever reason, I had continually bumped into people on the street or talked with them on the phone, and during our conversation they would say, "It's just another day."

Most times it would come after I asked them, "How are you doing?" I was beginning to think there was a lesson in this response for me personally and professionally.

"We don't have time to have 'just another day'" became a rallying point for me that spring in Bradenton at Pirate City. Our team had a strong first half in 2011 and had gotten the attention of a fan base that was walking into a new season with 18 consecutive losing seasons tied to them.

However, our second half was the opposite, and we added another year to the longest seasonal losing streak in North American sports history: 19.

My inspiration to our front office and team that camp was "We don't have time to have 'just another day.'" We were going to separate ourselves from that type of

Have a High Standard

thinking. We were going to find a way to get better each day in an area that we had underperformed in during 2011, such as playing a cleaner defense, driving in runners from third with fewer than two outs, or holding the opposing team's runners on base. We were going to focus on incremental improvement.

The players would be reminded weekly that we did not have time to waste or have a mentality that "it" could wait until tomorrow. And there was much "it" to improve on.

And really, no one has time to have "just another day" because there will be a point where we don't get any more days.

I encouraged our players, staff, and organization that everything would work more consistently and smoothly when we all made each day an opportunity for personal and professional development and improvement. Together we can actually make each other's job, and lives, easier rather than harder if we focus on making each day better, one day at a time.

Chapter 8

Finish Strong

We've all heard the quote, "It's not how you start; it's how you finish." I believe that's true. Starting well is important; however, what do you do when you don't start well? That's the deal-breaker or dealmaker. Learning how to adapt, improvise, and overcome is imperative.

I've encouraged every young high school player to finish strong with their academics. Finishing strong becomes a way of life. Once you've started a task, mission, or job, there will be multiple opportunities to bail out or quit.

Here is an example of finishing strong I learned in my teenage years.

I was complaining about having no money, so my dad had an easy answer . . . get a job. I wasn't big on occupational skills, and the few places I reached out to for work said no. So, my dad set me and a good friend up with a job.

I didn't ask any questions once he told me what the man was going to pay. We showed up at a trailer at a construction site and were informed we'd be riding in the back of a sanitary disposal truck cleaning out portable toilets. YUCK!

I worked the first week without issuing a word to my dad about the job. I learned quickly that tennis shorts and a polo shirt were not to be worn on the job. We worked all day long from 9 a.m. to 5 p.m. To say I stepped into a harsh dose of reality would be an understatement.

At the end of the second week working for Able Portable Toilets, I received my first check. It was the biggest check I had ever received in my life at that point. Still, the kind of work I was doing was gnawing on me, and one question remained: how did my dad think this work was going to be beneficial for me?

When I got home that day, I asked my dad to meet me in the garage for a conversation about work. I asked him what he thought this job was good for. I appreciated the money. But the smell at the end of the day was real, and the overall filth I dealt with on a daily basis was gross.

My dad calmly listened to my rant. When I finished, he looked at me and said, "It was the only job you were qualified for!" He also said, "Finish strong!" I did. Smell and all.

Hurdle-isms for Finishing Strong

- **Hurdle-ism 19:** Honor the exit.
- **Hurdle-ism 20:** Don't lose your stuff.

Hurdle-ism 19: Honor the Exit

Honor the exit.

That's the phrase I used when I was fired by the Rockies 19 months after being a part of the 2007 National League Championship team and the only Rockies team to make a World Series trip.

I can remember Dan O'Dowd calling me early in the morning on May 29, 2009, to set up a meeting. I pretty much figured my visit wasn't going to be about the lineup that night. We had been playing poorly across the board, and everything about our club seemed to be below average.

I arrived at Dan's house, and we sat down and had a very professional conversation about the challenges our ball club was going through and the organizational decision to replace me. I thanked him for the opportunity and shared that I would appreciate the time to call my staff and inform them as well as being able to schedule a time to meet with the team and then the media.

When I met with the players, I challenged them to finish the season strong because there was no reason that this team would not make the playoffs this year.

At the press conference with the media, I shared that I was thankful and grateful to Dick and Charlie Monfort, our ownership group, for their support. I was thankful for the support of our fan base. I also thanked the players for their efforts and shared how honored I was to be their manager. I would be forever grateful to Dan and Rockies president Keli McGregor for believing in me as well. Honor the exit.

There was no pointing fingers elsewhere or transferring the blame in other directions. I had encouraged our players at all levels for 15 years to be accountable and responsible, and I was not about to tear that down when a managerial firing sits squarely on the shoulders of the manager. Not anyone else.

Dan, Keli, and I had become close family friends as well as a very connected leadership group. In fact, I'm back with the Rockies now because I didn't burn bridges on the way out.

I work closely with our owner, Dick Monfort; our team president, Greg Feasel; and our general manager, Bill Schmidt. Dan and I remain very close friends. Keli has passed, but there aren't many days in which I don't think of him or talk with him.

Finish Strong

Another time I honored the exit was when I was fired after nine seasons as the Pittsburgh Pirates manager. It ended with a meeting in the manager's office at PNC Park three hours before the season finale and with two years left on my contract.

This is what I said to Stephen Nesbitt:

> "What I needed to understand throughout it all," Hurdle told *The Athletic* in a lengthy phone conversation over the weekend, "is there's a time when you show up, and there's a time when you're asked to leave. Not many people get to leave on their own accord. And that's OK. But you honor the exit."

I wasn't able to move it forward with the organization after that in significant fashion, but I knew I gave it everything I had while I was there. The coaches gave it everything they had. The players gave it everything they had. And there comes a moment in life when you mature and it's time to exit.

I had nothing to be ashamed of. I left the Pirates organization with my head held high and looked people in the eye on my way out. I honored the exit.

Hurdle-isms

Hurdle-ism 20: Don't Lose Your Stuff

When I was in Colorado, I got the opportunity to visit with some of the young players at our Colorado Rockies Youth Baseball Camp. When I introduced myself, I had three encouragements for the kids:

- Have fun by just *playing* the game.
- Be a good teammate by celebrating your teammates when they have success.
- Don't lose your stuff. Leave with what you came with. This will make your parents happy even if you don't get any hits.

Not long after sharing these three encouragements, I could not get the last one – "Don't lose your stuff" – out of my mind. There's no doubt about the importance of looking after yourself at all stages of life; however, for kids . . . well, they're kids.

Karla and I have felt the pain of the $45 Yeti thermos disappearing or the super-cool travel bag stuffed with gear being left behind. We can remind the kids all we want about gathering up their gear, but when they're young and something goes missing, parents are out a lot of time and money.

Once kids are old enough, parents can make them in charge of their gear and on the hook for the cost of replacing it if it is lost or "stolen." (I think I invented the "It was stolen" line about 1970. My dad usually straightened me out by finding what I had misplaced.)

That's when the magic usually starts to happen. Kids start to take responsibility of their gear and their lives and start to understand accountability.

Now, although I meant "stuff" in the physical sense when talking about kids, this Hurdle-ism of "Don't lose your stuff" has a more metaphorical meaning when we apply it to adults.

When I watch youth events, I eventually start watching the parents and try connecting them with their athletes. This is where the "Don't lose your stuff" approach really works or becomes unhinged. The verbal responses of parents are interesting. The body language is impressive. The occasional rant at a referee or umpire is entertaining for everyone . . . except for the referee or umpire.

Parents second-guessing the coach can be never-ending. I applaud all the parents who just show up, cheer, encourage everyone, and thank the coaching staff once the competition is over. This actually might be abnormal behavior because I see so much of the other.

My youngest kids, Maddie and Christian, have been involved in youth sports, and Karla and I have lived the challenges that can come with expectations. We've been blessed with watching the joy that comes from winning in competition and the heartache that losing can cause. As a family we've shared the importance of what being on a team means and the sacrifices that are made by all. We also reminded them of the importance of doing your best – whatever your best is that day.

Christian is the perfect son for me. He retired from baseball at the age of four. His retirement statement was "Dad, too intense. I'm out."

He remained a man of his word. He spent time exploring the worlds of karate, tennis, and crew. I have no clue about any of these sports, so I was saved from overcoaching my son or second-guessing the coach. Boy, I was sure glad I never had the chance to lose my stuff!

Finish Strong

Part V
Offseason

F inally, the offseason!

Every year the road to the offseason starts at one place and finishes at another. Each year provides different lessons learned, different challenges met, different relationships built, and all the victories and losses. It's a tough industry when the whole day is judged by the scoreboard and record, but that is our reality, so we keep working smart to do the right thing.

At the end of every season my first task was to head to our instructional league program and spend a week with all the coaches and players. As an organization, we'd always preach the importance of this league, so what better way to show all our players and coaches than for the Major League manager to spend time with them in uniform: to be present for the morning meetings, to watch the drill work, to watch the bullpens and batting practices, and to be in the dugout during the games?

I can remember being a young Royals player in the instructional league and watching manager Whitey Herzog show up unannounced. It was so incredibly cool that it left a mark on me, and when I became a Major League manager, there was no doubt in my mind how impactful spending a week at the instructional league could be.

When I get back home, I would give myself a solid period of time to just settle physically and mentally and allow my emotions and thoughts to slowly subside and try to find some balance as I transitioned back into my personal life and other responsibilities for the offseason.

After I feel settled, it's time to reflect. I've journaled for 15 years, so I have all my journals from my entire managerial career in Pittsburgh. I've got many folders full of pages of notes from my years in Colorado. Once I feel as if I've become a family member again, I pick pockets of time to review the previous season.

I just sit back and read my notes and jot down things that we did well, things we didn't do well, and things we might be able to improve on. As I mentioned previously in the book, it's a green light, red light, yellow light exercise. This takes some time, and I'm not in a rush to finish it.

I also extend the courtesy of not bothering or taxing my coaching staff with any responsibilities or phone calls unless absolutely necessary. They've seen enough of me and have definitely heard enough from me for the past nine months!

Chapter 9

We All Have Work to Do

We are all works in progress. One of the many lessons I've learned in the past 50 years is that the Golden Rule is still gold.

I first heard about the Golden Rule in vacation Bible school as a youngster. The idea that the world would be a better place if we would treat others as we would wish to be treated still has relevance today. I've found that the more I can be of service to others rather than demand to be served by others, the calmer and more peaceful my life is.

We all have daily schedules that can become complicated, and those schedules come with people, who at times can be very complicated and messy. When we drag our mess into our conversations with others, we drip toxic behavior on others. Or at least I know I do. Apologies for speaking for you.

I can remember going through the process of having both hips replaced in a three-month period. The months before were some of the most challenging I've ever encountered when dealing with pain. There were days when there was little relief and I was dependent on others for the simplest of tasks. Putting on socks and tying my shoes were the worst.

At home Karla was my caregiver, and at the stadium Jeff Banister, my bench coach with the Pirates, was my personal assistant for getting dressed and onto the field. As I attempted to navigate the days with daily prayer, acupuncture, and 90 minutes of physical therapy from Jeremiah Randall, one of our trainers, I would constantly remind myself to not push my pain on the people I would connect with.

Hurt people hurt people. I saw this play out a few times in my weak moments and bad days.

I also developed an awareness I never had before. I was able to look into people's eyes and see their pain or their hurt. Empathy and sympathy became walking partners with me as I tried to meet my daily demands.

Hurdle-isms for Having Work to Do

- **Hurdle-ism 21:** It's not about proving others wrong; it's about proving yourself right.

- **Hurdle-ism 22:** Model the behaviors you hope to instill in others.

Hurdle-ism 21: It's Not About Proving Others Wrong; It's About Proving Yourself Right

Man, did I have this Hurdle-ism backward for many years! From an athletic perspective, I didn't have many poor performances starting from Little League all the way through high school. Most of the time I was the best player on my team, and my abilities to play and hit were way above average. I was always a big fish in a small pond.

Then I was drafted in 1975 by the Kansas City Royals in the first round as the ninth pick in the nation.

From that point on, there were multiple times in my playing career when after a disappointing performance I had to deal with emotions I'd never processed before. Also, for the first time ever, I had to deal with fans booing and the media calling out my lackluster performance. I quickly realized I had become a small fish in a much bigger pond.

When I had a bad game, my quick fix was to tell myself, "That won't happen again." I really didn't attempt to analyze or honestly self-evaluate my approach or mechanics. I went straight to "I'll prove them all wrong."

In fact, my focus was on other people's evaluation of my performance and the vitriol that comes with that. In other words, I would let people whom I'd never ask for advice from to begin with control my emotional state moving forward. Brilliant, right?

I continued to have this ineffective mindset throughout my playing career. And trying to win over the crowd is the easiest and quickest way to not win over anyone, myself included.

It wasn't until 2005 when a conversation that I had with Bobby Cox, the Hall of Fame manager with the Atlanta Braves, opened my young manager's eyes and ears to a much better way of proving myself. Bobby reached out one day before a batting practice I was holding at Coors Field and asked me if we could meet the following afternoon. I was beside myself with excitement. I said yes, and we agreed on a time. Our meeting took place early the following afternoon.

Bobby shared some thoughts and encouragement with me and really took the time to commend my staff and the Colorado Rockies players about the way we were approaching the game and our level of energy. He shared

We All Have Work to Do

the importance of being consistent and cohesive during a rebuild period.

Bobby then pivoted and asked me if I listened to the talk radio shows after the game on the way home. I answered, "Yes." He said, "That's interesting."

He then asked if I read the newspaper the next day, especially the columnists' articles. I answered, "Yes." He said, "That's interesting."

He also asked if I listened to the game recap on the news at night. I answered, "Yes." Again, he said, "That's interesting."

He then said, "Clint, listen to me. Don't waste your time or energy listening to what other people think about your team or the job you're doing. You don't need to make sure they get it right. They'll say what they want to say, and they'll write what they want to write, and they're not going to ask you for your opinions or thoughts. Let your public relations guy read the newspapers and the notes and give you a heads-up on anything that you really need to know. Let him make your life easier."

He continued, "The only people you need to confide in and have conversations with are those in your organization and life who care about you and will tell you

Hurdle-isms

the truth. Trust your gut – unless it's indigestion – and follow what's best for you, and you'll prove yourself right."

I followed Bobby's advice from that day forward.

Many thanks to my two public relations directors, Jay Alves in Colorado and Jimmy Trdinich in Pittsburgh. They became my smoke detectors and made my job easier.

I'll be forever grateful to Bobby Cox for reaching out to me and sharing his experience and wisdom. I reached out to Bobby on a number of occasions after that day, and he was always gracious to listen to me and share his wisdom. Except for one time . . .

As we entered into extra innings in the 2008 All-Star Game at the iconic Yankee Stadium, I was the manager of the National League team, and our team was running out of pitching. I was asking my coaches, Lou Pinella and Buddy Black, for advice, and then I had a thought: our trainer for the game was Jeff Porter of the Braves. Jeff and I had spent a season of winter ball together in Venezuela and had become friends since then. I asked Jeff to give Bobby a call in the 12th inning so I could ask for some advice. Jeff made the call and handed me his phone.

I asked Bobby if he'd ever been in this position and what advice he might have. Bobby answered, "Looks like

99

We All Have Work to Do

you've got your hands full, kid. I'm going to get another glass of wine and sit back down in my recliner and see how this plays out."

I laughed out loud. Bobby helped downsize the people-pleaser in me dramatically. We all need someone in our lives who will tell us what we need to hear rather than what we might want to hear. I need a "human smoke detector" to help me remember to prove myself right.

Hurdle-ism 22: Model the Behaviors You Hope to Instill in Others

Boy, does this one come back to bite me frequently in my parenting skills. Karla uses this as a reminder for me because I sometimes get confused and bring the manager home instead of being the husband and the dad.

I can remember early on as the manager of the Rockies a conversation I had with our team president Keli McGregor. I asked Keli what his expectations of the manager were. He looked at me without blinking an eye and said, "Be managerial."

I replied, "OK, what does that mean?" He answered, "From this point on, you'll be representing our organization everywhere you go, in uniform and out. Everything you say and do will have a direct reflection upon the Colorado Rockies and on you as well as your family." Alrighty then. Enough said.

After much reflection and journaling out my thoughts, I realized this would make a solid leadership and teaching point to our team. I started sharing with our players and staff that our best way toward building connection, communication, and cohesion was to model the behaviors we

We All Have Work to Do

hoped to instill in others. We were all representing our team, ourselves, and our families.

With the name on the front of our jerseys – "Colorado" – we were representing our fan base and our organization. This included the surrounding communities and all the people who support our team, including our major sponsors.

The name on my back – "Hurdle" – represented my home. It represented the people who raised me and have supported me from birth until now. It represented the people who know me, not the ball player, and the people who live with me unconditionally.

In life, on or off the field, when you model the behavior you hope to instill in others, you hold yourself responsible and accountable for your actions and your words. We are all role models to someone, whether we like it or not. Do your best to give them someone to look up to.

So back to my parental skills. On more occasions than I can count, Karla has gently reminded me that our children might not always listen to what I say; however, they are always watching what I do.

And as most parents probably can attest, kids somehow seem to be most observant when we parents are not representing ourselves well. I'm not at my best in heavy traffic. Actually, I'm not at my best while waiting for any-thing. I'm not at my best when being called out by my kids on a promise I made a month ago and have since forgotten. I'm not at my best when I'm the only guy in the house with three women and three dogs. I'm not at my best when I hear a premature "Bingo" call at the Key Royale Club and Maddie yells out, "What the hell, lady?" because she just heard her dad mutter it (and not under-neath his breath).

And that's when my beautiful, smart, loving, and self-less wife grabs me by the ear and looks at me with those captivating brown eyes and says, "Model the behavior you hope to instill in others."

We All Have Work to Do

Chapter 10

Respect and Celebrate Others

For many years I felt a need to have others earn my respect, even though I was taught to respect my elders and figures of authority. I believed that I'd earn your respect and you'd earn mine. As I look back on it now it seemed to turn many encounters into confrontations.

If you performed well or acted well, then you had a chance for my respect, and I would eventually even applaud your efforts and cheer you on. As time passed, I came to the conclusion that life was much simpler and less messy if I treated others with respect from the start and I applauded their efforts just because it was the right thing to do. I did not need to be the judge and jury of their actions or intentions.

One of my realizations on my journey had been that many emotions can be contagious. Kindness, generosity, empathy, and positivity can all spark others when they are authentic and consistent.

Hurdle-isms for Respecting and Celebrating Others

- **Hurdle-ism 23:** Respect everyone, fear no one.

- **Hurdle-ism 24:** The tone and timing of what we say can be a dealmaker or a deal-breaker. Boom!

- **Hurdle-ism 25:** Celebrate others' success; when you celebrate others, you get to celebrate way more often.

Hurdle-ism 23: Respect Everyone, Fear No One

Five words. These words are very powerful and impactful when consistently demonstrated. You might wonder how you can respect everyone, especially the people you don't know.

That's how I thought for a long time. *You need to earn my respect. I don't just hand it out like Halloween candy. You're going to have to work for it.* But who made me in charge of the universe?

As I started seeing higher competition in baseball, I learned quickly that the players I was competing against were getting bigger and stronger. As you get older and keep succeeding in a sport, you go from being the best in your city or high school to playing against everybody who was the best in their city or high school.

This got my attention quickly and actually challenged my confidence. Fear usually shows up when there are unknowns. As you start playing Minor League baseball, there are unknowns every night: the field, the lights, the pitcher, their players, and so on.

Respect and Celebrate Others

I was fortunate to have two strong role models coach me early on in my professional development. Gary Blaylock was my first professional manager with the Kansas City Royals in Sarasota, which was the Rookie League. Gary had a physical presence and a blue-collar work ethic. Gary was a pitcher in his playing days, and it was amazing to me how much he knew about everything connected to the game.

There were days when I thought he must have been a drill sergeant somewhere. He did not waste words, and his attention to detail was impressive. He was a tremendous man and teacher of life and baseball. He would consistently remind us to respect everyone.

> "Respect the name on the front of the jersey. That's your new home. You are part of an organization. You are to represent the organization on and off the field. If you respect everyone on and off the field, you will put yourself in a much better position to be successful. Respect can be hard to earn, and it may take some time. It can also be lost quickly."

I can hear Gary sharing those words with us today . . . 50 years later. That man left a mark on me, and I'm thankful for his words.

Respect everyone. This is something I've carried into my daily life as well. There aren't many days when I don't learn something from someone or I was blessed with someone's experience or wisdom. I've watched so many people bless our family that I'll never take another person for granted or look down on their profession or skill set.

The other person I'm talking about was John Sullivan, my first full-season manager. After the Rookie League, the next step was Class A ball in Waterloo, Iowa. "Sully" was similar to Gary in that they both were veteran baseball men who loved every aspect of the game.

Sully was a catcher in his playing days; however, he had learned all about the entire game in his career. He was built like a catcher – not short but not tall. Barrel chested and strong, with really strong hands.

He let us know early in that there was no place for fear. Many of us were playing a complete season for the first time: April through August, more than 130 games. Most of us were far from home for the first time. Many were living on their own for the first time. I was all of the above.

Respect and Celebrate Others

Sully would say, "You're playing a game. The greatest game ever invented! There's no place for fear. It will hold you back. Go play like you were in the backyard when you were a kid."

I had a chance one day to show Sully I had no fear. Unfortunately, it came after a fly ball hit me in the face. I didn't get my glove up in time as I was backpedaling into the warning track and lost my footing. Bam! The next thing I know Sully and our trainer are looking over me. There was some blood and some pain; however, the embarrassment of what just happened were overriding everything.

Both men told me my nose was broken and I needed to go inside. I shared with them that was not an option. I was going to finish the inning and then go inside and access the damage. They both nodded and said OK. Once inside I went to the bathroom and looked in the mirror. My nose was bloodied, and it did not look like the nose I woke up with. It was bent to the right. I asked the trainer what we should do. He said bend it back. So I did. And then he yelled at me because he was the one who was supposed to bend it back.

Go figure. In all honesty. It was extremely painful. I then marched back to the dugout and told Sully I was good to go. He smiled sheepishly and said, "Fear nothing."

The moral of the story is that those two men each shared a thought that affected me for the rest of my life. When I started my next season, I just combined the two thoughts and turned them into one. Later on when I started coaching, they became a Hurdle-ism that I still use today.

Respect and Celebrate Others

Hurdle-ism 24: The Tone and Timing of What We Say Can Be a Dealmaker or a Deal-Breaker. Boom!

I have learned a lot of lessons in my life the hard way. There have been times in my life when I've stuck not only a foot in my mouth but the other foot as well as a couple of other body parts. Many times it was completely selfish on my part just to be cute or funny. Other times it was about being first with information and not really caring how accurate the information was. And still other times it was because I was replying without even hearing the other person's words first.

As I have matured personally and professionally, I have been fortunate to be mentored by a number of friends from my close inner circle. It's no coincidence that my hearing improved as did my teaching ability with the number of interactions I was having with other leaders and the number of conversations that I was engaging in with senior leader personnel.

Through trials and tribulations my timing and tone were the first things I considered before opening my mouth. I had a checklist to review on my content. Was it true? Did it add value? Was it relevant? Would it hurt others? Then I'd wait my turn to share and slowly articulate my thoughts without drama or theatrics – both of which I used to need for my own confidence.

It's been said that the person with the loudest voice has the least control of a conversation, and that used to fit me to a tee.

By using a calm and confident tone dripping with humility or humor, you might have a better chance of the person you're talking to actually wanting to hear what you have to say. Good timing when you share is a superpower.

My experience over the years has shown me that the elite leaders I spend time with are very good listeners. The tone of speech and the timing they use when interjecting thoughts or brainstorming ideas is calming, confident, convincing, and crystal clear. They always let you finish your thoughts and sentences before replying.

Have you ever had a conversation with someone who finishes your sentences for you? It drives me crazy. I've had a handful of friends over the years do just that. Rather than go on a rant or embarrass them, I wait for

Respect and Celebrate Others

an opportunity to bring this trait to their attention. Many times it's just nerves and they don't realize they're doing it.

Be a people "whisperer." Be someone others really want to talk to because they know you'll listen without judgment and you'll reply in a caring manner.

When your timing is bad, it will not matter a bit about the brilliant information you have to share. When your tone is overbearing, the only thought on the other person's mind is wondering when you are going to shut up and go away.

All of these points might or might not be valid with umpires. . . .

Hurdle-ism 25: Celebrate Others' Success; When You Celebrate Others, You Get to Celebrate Way More Often

It's called *mudita*, and it was my word for 2024.

Mudita is a concept of joy, particularly an especially sympathetic or vicarious joy – the pleasure that comes from delighting in other people's well-being. The traditional example of this mind state is the attitude of a parent observing a growing child's accomplishments.

The definition I've embraced is "expressive joy for the success of others." What a world we could live in if we would all try to do a little more celebrating of our friends' successes! Try it with your family, at work, in the gym, at church, at Bingo, at school, and anywhere you are connecting with others. On every team you'll ever play on. In every community and neighborhood you will live in.

This was a pivot for me at an early age. It didn't happen naturally. Playing sports, I often based my self-esteem and self-confidence on my own personal performance rather than on the team outcome. If I had a good day and the team lost, it was alright. If I had a bad performance and the team won, I had work to do. The fact we won didn't override the expectations I had for myself, which were more important than anything else.

As my career in pro ball took shape, I was able to watch and experience what being a good teammate was all about. At times it can be difficult to explain what's going on in the clubhouse and on the field; however, you know it when you see it and feel it. Let me try to explain and name names.

Mudita for the Tidewater Tides

One of my most memorable seasons from a team standpoint was in 1983 at Triple A with the Tidewater Tides. We were an affiliate of the New York Mets organization, and we were a blended team of players heading to the Major Leagues or having been sent down from the Big Leagues. It was an array of players and emotions – happy, sad, hopeful, jaded, excited, disappointed – but basically all of us were hungry to prove something.

We were managed by Davey Johnson and coached by Al Jackson, who were both very good Major League performers. Both men had vast knowledge and experience to share and were genuinely interested in the players and coaching them up on the field. You couldn't have picked two better men for this team.

The team itself was loaded with men who would all play in the Major Leagues again. We had pitching: Ron Darling, Walt Terrell, Tim Leary, Tom Gorman, and Dwight Gooden would join us later. We had talent all over the diamond as well: Mike Fitzgerald and Ronn Reynolds caught. Gary Rajsich, Wally Backman, Ron Gardenhire, and I were in the infield. Marvel Wynne, Rusty Tillman, Gil Flores, and Darryl Strawberry were in the outfield.

This group played together, fought together, and celebrated together. We started off slow as we were all figuring out our roles and responsibilities. A little past mid-season it all came together and we never looked back. These were some of the best days of my career in baseball, and it all happened in Triple A with a group of men who respected each other and celebrated each other's success like they were their own.

Muditā for the Colorado Rockies

I was fortunate to get a front-row seat to some professional muditā in Colorado in 2007. That's one of the years

Respect and Celebrate Others

that will always be etched in the forefront of my mind because of the joy that team brought to its fan base, community, and organizational employees.

In Colorado I witnessed a group of predominantly homegrown players mature together on and off the field. We met the demands of the season all year long and absolutely caught fire in September and October. We birthed the term *Rocktober* that still brings smiles to many faces in the Rocky Mountain region.

We won 21 of our last 22 games. The play-in game versus the San Diego Padres was and still is one of the most iconic and thrilling postseason games ever. We swept the Philadelphia Phillies in the National League Division Series and the Arizona Diamondbacks in the National League Championship Series. We were a team that started the season hoping we would win and turned into a team that started expecting to win, and by the end we didn't think we could lose.

So many good, unselfish players complemented one another daily. We were led by the face of the franchise, Todd Helton. The team was a blueprint of the Rockies mantra to be a "draft and develop" organization. Troy Tulowitzki brought a much-needed edge to our team that

Hurdle-isms

became contagious. Matt Holliday and Brad Hawpe were cornerstones, as was Garret Atkins. Yorvit Torrealba and Kaz Matsui brought energy every day. Willy Taveras was the speed merchant who changed games. Corey Sullivan and Ryan Spilborghs were incredibly valuable as role players down the stretch.

Our pitching staff was the engine that kept everything else going. We had a combination of young and old with all different arm angles and pitches. We had two young starting pitchers in Ubaldo Jimenez and Franklin Morales. We had a superb competitor and sinker ball pitcher in Aaron Cook and another guy with big guts in Josh Fogg. Our ace was Jeff Francis. A host of men filled in our rotation.

We had a lockdown bullpen that shortened the game to our advantage throughout the season. Two different men closed games for us during the season. Brian Fuentes closed for us the first part of the season, and Manny Corpas closed the back half. Matt Herges, Jeremy Affeldt, and LaTroy Hawkins all played important roles in setting up our closers. This group was dependable and reliable, and you can't ask any more from a bullpen.

All these men showed up every day and were solely focused on doing whatever was asked of them to help

Respect and Celebrate Others

us win a game. They celebrated with each other, and they celebrated with each other often. They showed our coaching staff and me what muditā looked like.

Muditā for the Pittsburgh Pirates

I also saw muditā in Pittsburgh in 2013, which was the other year that I had the best seat in the house to watch a group of players become a team – a team that eliminated a lot of ghosts from seasons past. The Pirates had put together a string of 20 consecutive losing seasons, which at the time was a North American record for futility.

Two of those years were on my watch. For two years the core group of this team developed a mental toughness and a physical grit that became building blocks for the future.

By 2013 our front office, led by Neal Huntington and Kyle Stark, had strategically added personnel to a good young core. Andrew McCutchen, Neil Walker, Pedro Alvarez, and Starling Marte were coming into their own in the league. Jordy Mercer eventually took over shortstop. Clint Barmes solidified the infield and the clubhouse. Veterans Francisco Liriano and Jason Grilli gave the team some edge, and when A. J. Burnett and Russell Martin were acquired, we had way more than edge.

The bullpen was incredible. Our closer was Jason Grilli, and the players who got the ball to him were all having fantastic seasons. From Tony Watson, Jeanmar Gomez, Mark Melancon, Justin Wilson, and Joe Blanton, protecting the lead was their business, and they did it as well as any bullpen in the league. During the season Gerrit Cole, Justin Morneau, Marlon Byrd, and Wandy Rodriguez were added, and it was a full-blown game-on mentality.

A swagger started to take place in our clubhouse, dugout, bullpen, and our play on the field. We weren't backing down from anyone. This team rebonded the city of Pittsburgh with its ballclub. The Pirates were back and all in. Raising the Jolly Roger was an exclamation point at the end of each game.

Our team developed a ritual before the lineup exchange of putting together a homemade bandstand and drum section. These men found a way to enter the game loose and confident, and the dance changed daily.

The coaching staff and I just looked on and smiled – a bunch of grown-up kids getting ready to play for each

Respect and Celebrate Others

other. They played their backsides off and celebrated each other's success like no team I've ever been a part of.

As I finish writing this book, I want to share a thought on perspective. Do you have any idea how many men in the history of Major League Baseball have been to the World Series as a player, coach, and manager?

Hmmmm. Me neither. My guess is it's a small number. You know what's an even smaller number? The number of men who have gone to the World Series as a player, coach, or manager and finished second! I can't wait for my fourth trip. I've heard the fourth time is a charm!

About the Author

Clint Hurdle has spent 48 seasons in professional baseball, where he has won a total of 1,269 games as a manager between the Colorado Rockies and Pittsburgh Pirates. The 1,269 wins rank 38th all-time in managerial history.

In 1975, Hurdle was selected ninth overall in the June draft by the Kansas City Royals. At the age of 20, he made his Major League debut with the Royals on September 18, 1977. On March 20, 1978, he graced the cover of *Sports Illustrated* with the headline "This Year's Phenom."

Hurdle managed the Rockies across parts of eight seasons from 2002 to 2009. In 2007, Hurdle led the Rockies to its first-ever World Series appearance as the club captured its first National League pennant. The 2007 club won 11 straight games in September and 21 of 22 games leading to the World Series before falling to the Boston Red Sox.

On November 15, 2010, Hurdle was appointed as the 39th manager of the Pittsburgh Pirates, where he helped to "rebond" and "reconnect" the city of Pittsburgh with a team that went on to make three straight postseason appearances from 2013 to 2015. During his tenure with the Pirates, he was named the 2013 National League Manger-of-the-Year, while winning a total of 735 games, which ranks fourth on the club's all-time managerial wins list.

Recently Hurdle returned to Colorado as a special assistant to the general manager prior to the 2022 season. In this role, Hurdle assists across all areas of baseball operations, primarily in player development and scouting.

Hurdle has demonstrated his passion to make a difference in the communities he and his family have been a part of in Denver and Pittsburgh through his time and charity in supporting many causes, including as the national spokesperson and member of the board of the Prader-Willi Syndrome Association. He also sits on the board of directors for the Major League Baseball Players Alumni Association.

Hurdle makes his home in the city of Holmes Beach, Florida, with his wife, Karla, and is the proud father of three children: Ashley, Madison, and Christian.

Acknowledgments

There are many fingerprints on success, and I hope this book is proof of that.

I need to thank the following people:

Karla – God has shown me how much He loves me by placing you in my life and you choosing to be my partner. Your patience and belief in me has been constant throughout our relationship. You saw the person I could be more than 30 years ago and challenged me to become the best version of myself. There is no me today without you. As you love to say . . . "I'm still learning."

I love you, Karla June.

Ashley – We have more in common than either one of us realized until we both sought help and started living our best lives. How about us? You've become the best daughter I could have in your own unique and authentic way, and hopefully I've become the father you've needed. You continue to create a positive wake everywhere you go and your zest for life is contagious. I love you, Ashley.

Maddie – You are our angel without wings. When God chose us to be your parents, little did we know how much you'd teach us about life, yourself, and the Prader-Willi Syndrome community. Who loves dogs more than you? I love you, MoonPie.

Christian – You have been an incredible son. I'm behind you each step you take on your journey. Your lens on life is so creative I can't wait to see what you're going to accomplish. And you love so much it puts a smile on all our hearts. I love you, C-Man.

Mom – There's not been one day that you haven't believed in me or loved me unconditionally. Even when I was hard to love. Thank you for catching my early pitching practices. Seems like you've been my first responder forever. I love you, Mother.

Wiley Publishing – Shout-outs to Shannon, Zachary, Michelle, Amanda, and especially Kim (she gets me!) for walking me through this process and helping me share experiences full of encouragement, strength, and hope. Along with a few laughs.

Jon Gordon – You came up with the term *Hurdleisms* and then encouraged me to bring them to life. Your mentorship over the years as well as your nudging through the writing of the book were invaluable.

Dave Burchett – You initiated my leaning into "writing a book and telling my story." Your servant's heart and grace has not gone unnoticed, and I believe we will have a story to tell as well.

Acknowledgments

Index

131

Index